LEARNING RESOURCES CENTER
UNIVERSITY OF WYOMING LIBRARIES
LARAMIE, WY 82071

DATE DUE			
JUL 0 6 1993			
OCT 0 6 1993			
MAY 3 1 1994			
JUN 1 1 1998			
NOV 2 0 1998			
DEC 1 3 1999			
NOV 2 3 2000			
DEC 1 2 2003			
FEB 2 5 2005			
MAY 2 7 2011			

HIGHSMITH # 45220

WITHDRAWN

E
Plu

© Franklin Watts 1990

Franklin Watts Inc.
387 Park Avenue South
New York, N.Y. 10016

Library of Congress Cataloging-in-Publication Data
Pluckrose, Henry Arthur.
   Clean it! / Henry Pluckrose.
     p.   cm. — (Ways to)
   Summary: Introduces the many words associated with cleaning in household, industrial, and natural settings.
   ISBN 0-531-14063-6
   1. House cleaning—Terminology—Juvenile literature.
2. Industrial housekeeping—Terminology—Juvenile literature.
[1. House cleaning—Terminology. 2. Industrial housekeeping—Terminology.] I. Title. II. Series: Pluckrose, Henry Arthur. Ways to.
TX324.P58   1990
648'.5'014—dc20   89-49441
                                                        CIP AC

Editor: Ruth Thomson
Design: K & Co

Additional photographs:
Chris Fairclough Colour Library,
Hutchison Library,
ZEFA.
With thanks to Braun (UK) Ltd,
Hoover and Hotpoint.

Printed in Italy by G. Canale S.p.A., Turin

All rights reserved

Ways to....
CLEAN *it!*

Henry Pluckrose
Photography by Chris Fairclough

FRANKLIN WATTS
New York • London • Sydney • Toronto

When you wash, the soapy lather cleans your skin.

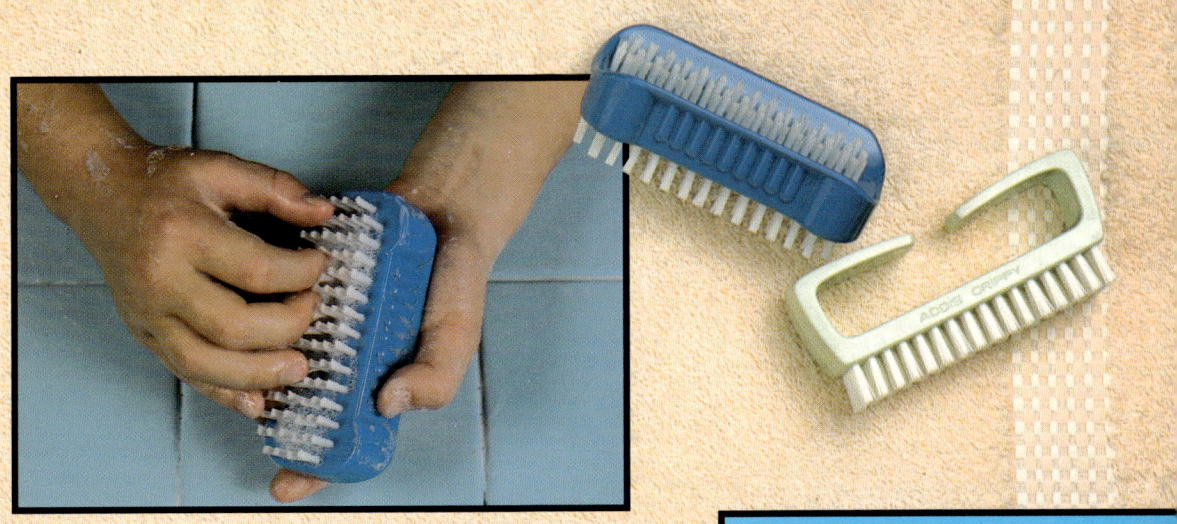

Rubbing and scrubbing help the soap remove the dirt.

Your teeth chew food to make it easier to swallow and digest. Some food stays in your mouth.

Unless it is brushed away, it will rot your teeth.

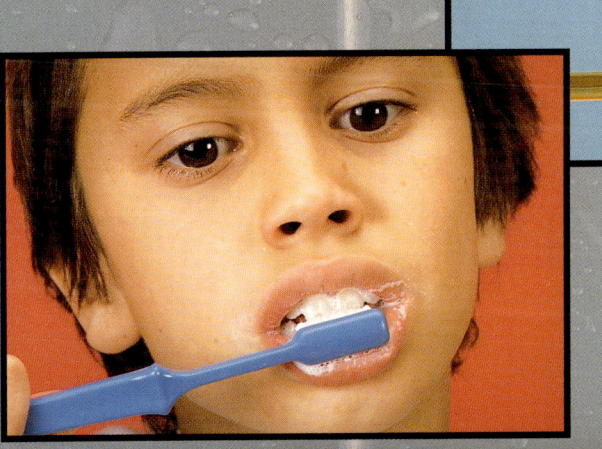

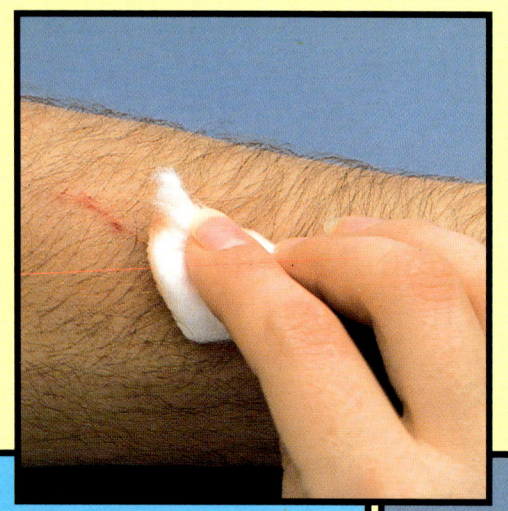

Harmful bacteria live on dirty skin. Dirt in a cut can keep it from healing. We put a bandage on a cut to keep it clean.

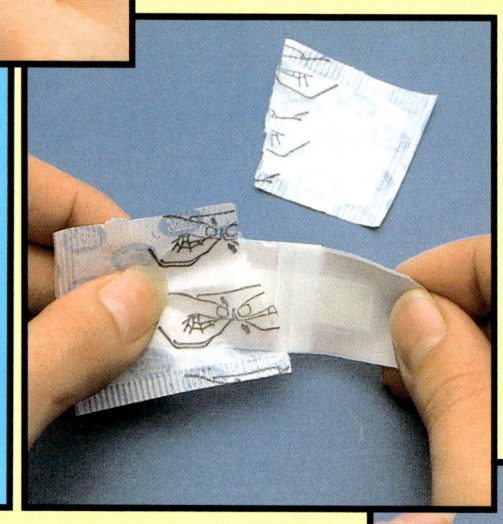

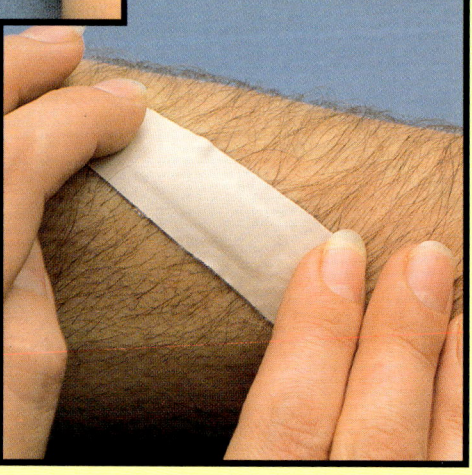

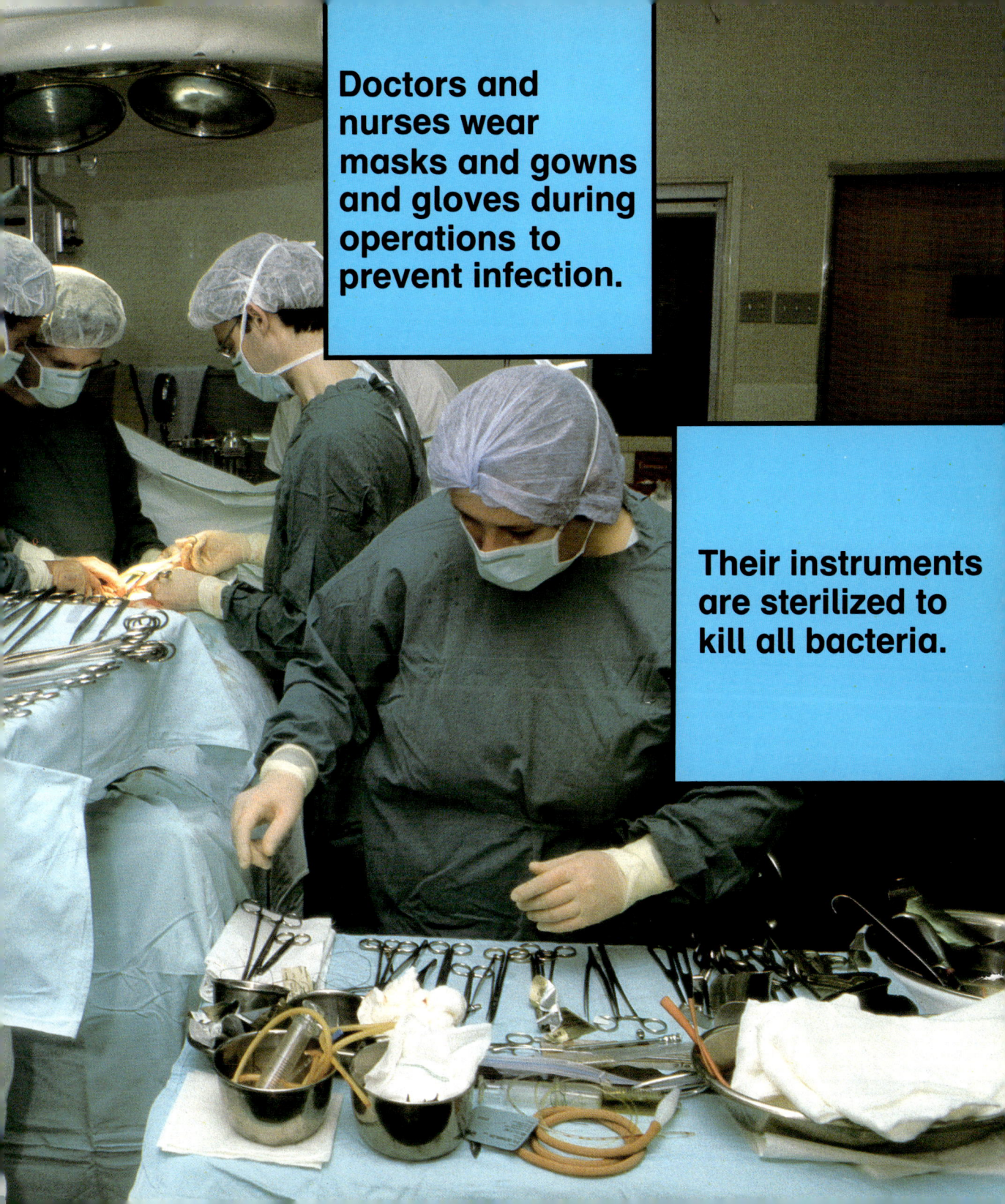

Clean bodies feel best in clean clothes. Detergents loosen dirt from clothes. Water washes it away.

What else happens to the clothes before you can wear them?

Your home needs to be kept clean too.

Harmful bacteria have to be kept away from food. Plates, knives and forks are clean before we use them.

We need to keep our world clean too.

Cleaning is hard work. These machines make the work easier.

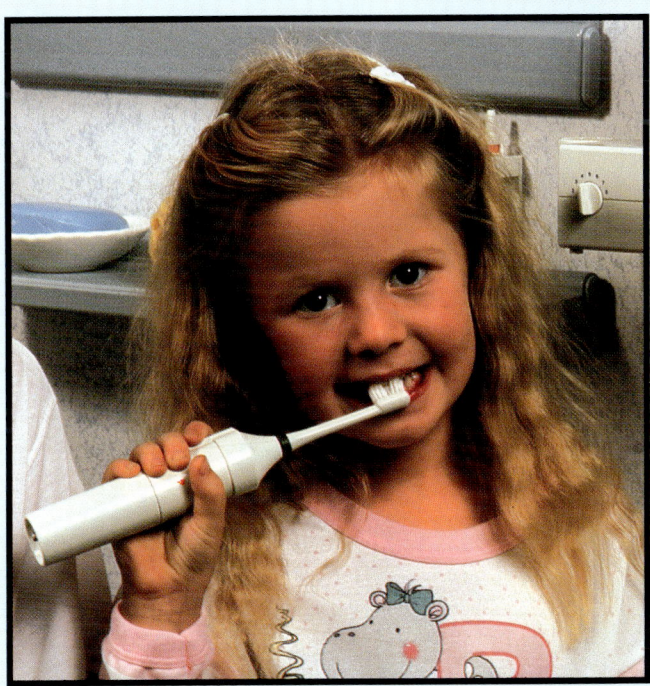

What are these used to clean?

Some things to do

- Make bubbles with your hands. You can do this in the bath.

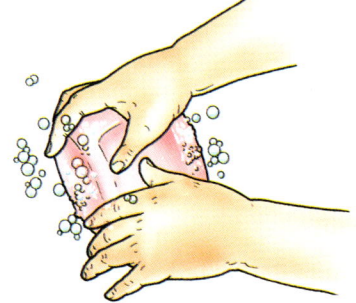

1. Make your hands very soapy.

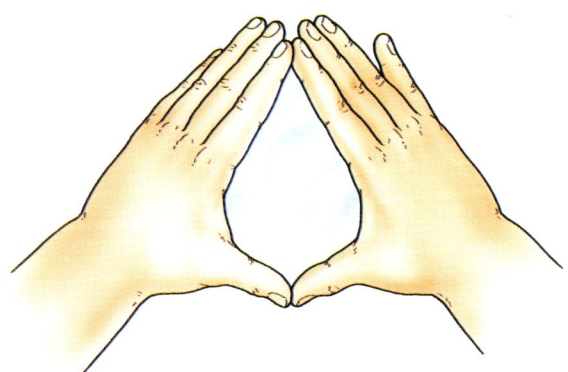

2. Carefully form a square with your thumbs and forefingers, trapping a film of soapy water between them.

3. Blow gently to make a bubble.

- Take your empty glass bottles to your local bottle bank so that they can be recycled. Broken bottles are crushed and used to make more glass. Find out how other things can be recycled.

● Offer to help with the washing up. Try washing a greasy plate with just cold water. Now wash it with hot water and dishwashing liquid. What is the difference?

● Shine a coin. You will need
   – some newspaper
   – a dirty coin
   – silver-cleaning cloth
   – paper towels

● Next time you visit a supermarket take a pencil and paper. Write down the names of the different cleaning products. Make a list of the words they use on each package to describe what the product does. Think about why you would choose one product rather than another.

Rub the coin with small pieces of the cloth. Finish it off by rubbing it with paper. The coin will be bright as new.

Words about cleaning

basin	scrub
bath	shampoo
bright	shine
broom	sink
brush	soak
bubbles	soap
cloth	sparkle
detergent	sponge
dishwasher	sweep
foam	toothbrush
gleam	toothpaste
lather	towel
mop	vacuum cleaner
polish	wash
pumice stone	wash cloth
rinse	washing machine
rub	

LEARNING RESOURCES CENTER
UNIVERSITY OF WYOMING LIBRARIES
LARAMIE, WY 82071